A Robbie Reader

Class Trip
CHICAGO

Kathleen Tracy

PUBLISHERS

P.O. Box 196
Hockessin, Delaware 19707
Visit us on the web: www.mitchelllane.com
Comments? email us: mitchelllane@mitchelllane.com

Mitchell Lane
PUBLISHERS

Boston • **Chicago** • New York City
Philadelphia • San Antonio • San Diego
Seattle • St. Augustine • Washington, D.C.

Printing   1 2 3 4 5 6 7 8 9

Library of Congress
Cataloging-in-Publication Data

Tracy, Kathleen.
  Class trip Chicago / by Kathleen Tracy.
    p. cm. — (A Robbie reader)
  Includes bibliographical references and index.
  ISBN 978-1-58415-881-3 (library bound)
  1. Chicago (Ill.)—Description and travel—Juvenile literature. 2. Chicago (Ill.)—History—Juvenile literature. I. Title.
  F548.52.T73 2010
  917.73'11—dc22

                           2010000517

                            PLB

CONTENTS

CHICAGO

Lake Shore Drive was originally built so wealthy Chicagoans in the late 1800s could walk along Lake Michigan or ride in their carriages. Today, it is part of a main highway from the South Side to the upper North Side of the city.

Right: This is the official White House photograph of Chicago native Michelle Obama.

Chapter 1

A Field Trip, Chicago-Style

Haley O'Malley shivered as she put on her school uniform. She couldn't believe how cold it was. Yesterday had been a beautiful, warm March day. She rode her bike after school wearing shorts. Then, last night around dinnertime, a cold wind started blowing, pushing big black clouds across the sky and whistling under the doors. Haley had woken up in the middle of the night to the sound of **sleet** hitting her bedroom window. It was now cold enough that her boxer, Timmy, had slept curled against her.

Mrs. O'Malley poked her head into Haley's room to be sure Haley was awake and getting ready. "Better get downstairs and eat your breakfast if you want to be on time." Haley gave her mom the same look she always did whenever the subject of being late for school came up.

After Haley had finished her cereal and brushed her teeth, her mom looked up from her own breakfast and checked the kitchen clock. "You sure you don't want a ride to school?"

Chicago

Illinois

SUB STATION

400 m
0,3 mi

Lake Michigan

W. Division St.
W. Elm St.
W. Hill St.
Seward Park
Newberry Library
E. Oak St.
W. Oak St.
E. Walton St.
John Hancock Center
W. Chestnut St.
E. Chestnut St.
Outer Harbor
Loyola University of Chicago
Armory
Water Tower
E. Chicago Ave.
W. Chicago Ave.
Moody Bible Institute
Northwestern University
Water Filtration Plant
W. Huron St.
E. Huron St.
Peace Museum
Terra Museum
Olive Park
W. Ontario St.
Museum of Contemporary Art
E. Ontario St.
Time Life Building
Lake Point Tower
W. Grand Ave.
E. Grand Ave.
Chicago Maritime Museum
Navy Pier
W. Hubbard St.
Tribune Tower
NBC Tower
Merchandise Mart
Wrigley Building
Equitable Building
Children's Museum
Centennial Fountain
W. Carroll Ave.
Marina City
E. Wacker Dr.
Chicago
W. Wacker Dr.
State of Illinois Center
Illinois Center
W. Randolph St.
Daley Center
Prudential Building
Amoco Building
City Hall & Co. Bldg.
Public Library
E. Randolph St.
Washington
Civic Opera House
St. Brunswick Plaza
Chicago Exchange
First National
Carson Pirie Scott
W. Monroe St.
E. Monroe St.
Union Station
U. S. Gypsum
Art Institute
W. Jackson Blvd.
Sears Tower
Orchestra Hall
Federal Center
E. Jackson Dr.
Board of Trade
Midwest Stock Exchange
Grant
290 Eisenhower Expwy.
W. Congress Pkwy.
Buckingham Fountain
Lake Shore Drive
Park
Columbia College
Lake
Spertus Museum
E. Balbo Dr.
Chicago
W. Polk St.
Harbor
Dearborn Station
E. 8th St.
W. Taylor St.
Logan Monument
E. 9th St.
Michigan
Chicago Fire Dept. Academy
E. 11th St.
Shedd Aquarium
W. Roosevelt Rd.
E. Roosevelt Rd.
Adler Planetarium
Field Museum of Natural History
Solidarity Dr.
E. 13th St.
Soldier Field
Burnham Park
E. 14th St.
Chicago
W. 15th St.

"No way," Haley said, zipping her jacket. "Klein texted and is waiting for me." Klein Argonosky was Haley's best friend and next door neighbor.

"Okay." Haley's mom smiled and kissed the top of her daughter's head. "Don't forget your cap. And no snowball fights."

"I won't," Haley promised, slinging her backpack across her shoulder. She found her cap on the floor of the closet and pulled it low over her ears. She stopped in the living room to feed her goldfish and then headed out the front door. She stopped and took a deep breath through her nose, enjoying the feeling of the cold. The entire front yard was covered with fluffy white flakes of snow. The sky was still cloudy, making the day look like a black-and-white photo.

Chicago is in northeastern Illinois at the southernmost tip of Lake Michigan. It is close to Wisconsin and Indiana. Its location has helped make this area into a large metropolitan region.

A snowball whizzed by her head. She turned and saw Klein on the sidewalk grinning. Haley bent down and scooped a handful of snow. From the house, Haley heard her mom yell, "No snowball fights!"

"Don't worry," Haley promised. She molded the snow into a tightly packed ball and threw it at the mailbox. It hit with a loud clank and the snowball exploded into a shower of icy white dust. Haley wished they had time to make a snowman, but school started in fifteen minutes. By the time they reached St. Bridget's, it had started raining, melting the snow. Now, Haley thought, she would probably have to wait until next winter to make a snowman.

Haley sat behind Klein in the row closest to the window. The first class on Mondays, called American Herstory, was about the roles played by women in U.S. history. But their teacher, Ms. Thomason, told her students they wouldn't need their textbooks.

"We're going to do something different this week," she explained. "We're going to study a city." Mrs. Thomason taped a map of Illinois on the chalkboard. The top east corner of the state was next to Lake Michigan. Chicago was shaded red and took up most of the area next to the lake. Everyone in the class had been to Chicago. It was less than an hour away from Hobart, Indiana, where they lived.

"For everything you know about Chicago," the teacher said, "there's so much more you don't. There's a lot of history that's been forgotten."

Klein raised his hand. "Like what?"

ALLS AND ROCK GARDEN IN OLSON
RROUNDING OLSON RUG FACTORY,
Y AT PULASKI (CRAWFORD) CHICAGO

OLSON RUG CO.

It took 200 workers more than six months to build Olson's Park. Once it was finished, it became one of the most popular places for families in Chicago to go on weekends.

Mrs. Thomason leaned against her desk. "Like, there used to be a waterfall right in the middle of Chicago."

Klein frowned **skeptically** (SKEP-tik-lee). "But there aren't any mountains in Chicago."

"Which is why in 1935 a man named Walter Olson built one himself," she explained. "Mr. Olson owned a rug **manufacturing** (man-yoo-FAAK-chur-eeng) company and wanted to make the area around the factory nicer. So he planted a huge garden with thousands of flowers along with pine, spruce, and juniper trees. He also put in a rock garden, a duck pond, and a 35-foot waterfall." Mrs. Thomason then passed around some pictures of the park.

"Is it still there?" Haley asked.

"The factory closed and was sold in 1965. The park stayed open until 1978, when it was taken apart and turned into a parking lot."

Several students groaned, upset at hearing the park was gone forever. Mrs. Thomason told them not to be sad. "That's the best part of studying history," she said. "By learning about things like Olson's Park,

Did You Know?

Riverview Park

Riverview Park was once considered the world's largest amusement park. Opened in 1904, it was best known for its roller coasters. The fastest were The Bobs, which reached 65 miles per hour, and the Fireball, which reportedly could reach 90 mph in perfect weather conditions. Many coaster fans claim the Fireball was the fastest coaster ever built. Riverview closed in 1967.

Navy Pier juts way out into Lake Michigan from downtown Chicago. It is a historic landmark with plenty of space for carnivals, concerts, and other special events.

it stays alive. It also helps you understand how Chicago became the great city it is today."

Their history assignment for the week, she said, was to learn as much about the city as possible and present the reports on Friday. "That way, you'll have even more fun when we take a class trip to Chicago next Monday."

This last bit of news came as a real surprise. Excited about the upcoming trip to Chicago, the students spent the rest of the history class working on their Chicago subjects. Haley looked out the window, thinking how blue Lake Michigan would look along Chicago's lakefront. The last snowfall of the season was now forgotten!

CHICAGO

Jacques Marquette meets with Native people during the time of his explorations of the Great Lakes region, including present-day Chicago.

Right: Jean Baptiste Point du Sable founded the first non-Native settlement in Chicago in 1781.

Second City— Historical Chicago

On Friday, the first thing Mrs. Thomason did was get all the reports on Chicago's history together. Here are some of the things the students learned.

Prior to the arrival of European settlers, present-day northeast Illinois and southeast Wisconsin near Lake Michigan was home to many Native tribes. In 1673, two French Canadians—explorer Louis Jolliet and priest Jacques Marquette—were brought to the area by Native people. Jolliet and other French explorers such as Henri Joutel thought the spot made an ideal trade location. It was situated between two rivers, now known as the Chicago and Des Plaines Rivers.

The area came to be called *Chicago*, the French **adaptation** (aa-dap-TAY-shun) of the Miami-Illinois word *shikaakwa*, meaning "wild onion," which grew **abundantly** (ah-BUN-dunt-lee) throughout the region. The first non-Native settlement was founded in 1781 by Jean Baptiste Point du Sable. A black man who had been born in what is now Haiti of mixed French and Haitian **descent**, du Sable built the first permanent, non-Native house in what is today Chicago at the mouth of the Chicago River.

The house had five bedrooms and was considered a mansion for its time. He established a very successful trading post and later married the daughter of a Potawatomi chief. His granddaughter, born in 1796, was the first baby born in Chicago.

In 1795, the Chicago area was given to the United States by local Native people in the Treaty of Greenville. The military used the land to build Fort Dearborn in 1803. In 1837, Chicago was **incorporated** (in-KOR-pur-ay-ted) as a city. The population was 4,000. The arrival of the railroads in the 1840s brought thousands more.

Chicago in 1779
(Then Called Eschikago)
Showing the Cabin of Jean Baptiste Point de Saible (Colored)
The First Permanent Settler

Chicago In 1779. On the left is the cabin of Jean Baptiste Point du Sable, the first permanent settler of the city. A portrait of du Sable is on the lower right. Note the cabin and Native dwellings on either side of the river.

In 1855, the exploding population prompted the city to build the first city-wide sewer system in the United States. By 1870 more than 300,000 people lived in Chicago, which was then the busiest railroad city in the world. Then disaster struck.

During the summer and fall of 1871, Chicago's normally **humid** climate was unusually dry. Plants withered and trees were parched. Even the buildings, all built with wood, seemed to creak in thirst.

At a little after 9:00 P.M. on the night of Sunday, October 8, a fire started in a barn owned by Patrick and Catherine O'Leary. It spread quickly. Making matters worse, the fire department went to the wrong

Three views of the aftermath of the Great Fire of 1871. Left: Residents examine the devastation in the central downtown area known as the Loop. Center: The historic Chicago Water Tower, on the city's Near North Side, was one of the few buildings in the fire zone that survived the fire. Right: These townhouses, in the city's Near North Side Gold Coast district, are among the many buildings put up following the fire.

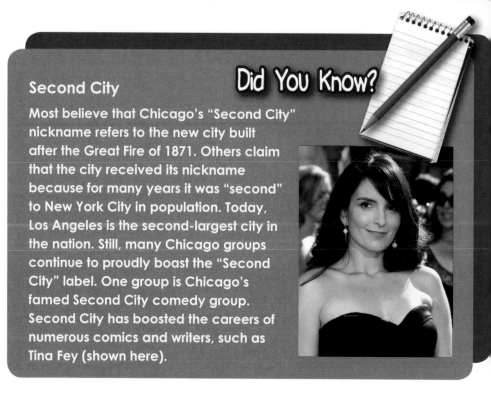

Did You Know?

Second City

Most believe that Chicago's "Second City" nickname refers to the new city built after the Great Fire of 1871. Others claim that the city received its nickname because for many years it was "second" to New York City in population. Today, Los Angeles is the second-largest city in the nation. Still, many Chicago groups continue to proudly boast the "Second City" label. One group is Chicago's famed Second City comedy group. Second City has boosted the careers of numerous comics and writers, such as Tina Fey (shown here).

address. When they finally showed up at the O'Leary barn, the fire was out of control. The fast-burning blaze consumed every building in its path. The fire burned for nearly two days until a rainstorm helped extinguish it.

The damage was devastating. Over 17,000 buildings were destroyed. The entire business district was reduced to ash. An estimated 100,000 people were homeless, and 300 lost their lives. The well-known story about Mrs. O'Leary's cow starting the fire was first reported by a reporter who later admitted making it up because he thought it made a good story. What or who started the fire remains a mystery.

Many of the nation's leading architects helped rebuild Chicago. The city recovered quickly, and in

1893 hosted the World's Columbian Exposition, better known as the Chicago World's Fair. The world's first Ferris wheel was introduced at the Fair.

By the early 1900s, Chicago's population was 1.7 million—and it just kept getting bigger. Chicago was a popular destination for European immigrants, especially from Ireland and Poland. The city's black population also swelled. The influx of African Americans and immigrants sometimes resulted in ethnic tensions, but Chicago's diversity has also made the city the artistic, culturally vibrant **metropolis** (meh-TRAH-puh-liss) it is today.

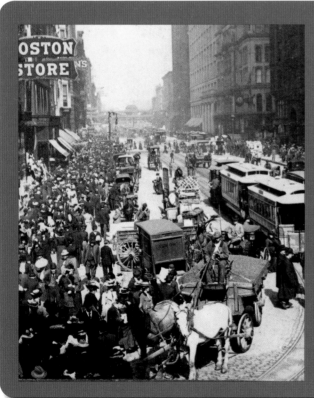

Millionaire businessman Potter Palmer turned State Street into Chicago's main shopping district. He did this by arranging for expensive department stores like Marshall Field's to be built on his land. The design for these early skyscrapers and other department store buildings became known as the Chicago School of Architecture.

This view of Chicago shows the Chicago River and Lake Michigan as two of the city's dominant natural features.

Right: This Canada goose is one of the many **species** of birds that **migrate** through Chicago every fall and spring.

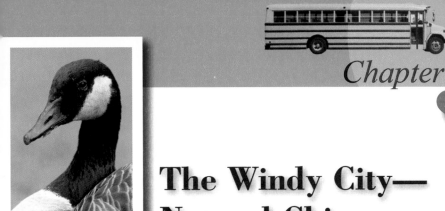

Chapter 3

The Windy City— Natural Chicago

Chicago is part of the Great Lakes **Plains**, a lowland area that stretches from Wisconsin to Ohio along Lake Michigan. The most common features are small hills, **marshes**, lakes, and rivers. The soil of the Plains is very **fertile** (FUR-tuhl), and the countryside surrounding Chicago was filled with thousands of grain and dairy farms. As the city grew, however, the land was developed for houses and businesses. Today there are still a few commercial farms. But the demand for organic food and lean meats like ostrich and buffalo has created a new business. Individual "farmettes" located in the suburbs are growing produce and raising livestock and selling them at local farmers' markets.

The growing season in Chicago is limited by its climate. Unlike southern California and Florida, which have mild weather year round, Chicago has very distinct seasons. In the summer, it is hot and humid. Thunderstorms are common, so crops grow plentifully. Fall is usually dry, with cool days and chilly nights.

Winters can be brutally cold. Wind blowing off of Lake Michigan makes the air feel colder than it really is. On January 20, 1985, the coldest day in the city's history, the temperature was –27°F, but the "windchill factor" made it feel like it was –83°F. Snow usually falls in sizeable amounts in Chicago in January and February. It's not unusual to have snow fall in March. Spring weather doesn't last long, and by June the summer temperatures are back.

Winter: Ice skating in downtown Chicago
Summer: The Oak Street Beach on Lake Michigan

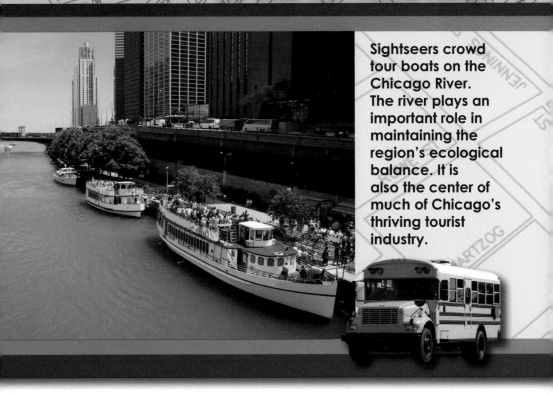

Sightseers crowd tour boats on the Chicago River. The river plays an important role in maintaining the region's ecological balance. It is also the center of much of Chicago's thriving tourist industry.

The two most important landforms in the Chicago area are the Chicago River and Lake Michigan. In 1848 the Illinois and Michigan Canal was opened, connecting the city to the Mississippi River. Ninety-three miles long, the canal began at the Chicago River in South Chicago and ran to the Illinois River. From there boats could make their way to the Mississippi. The canal made Chicago a vital trade route. Passenger boats also used the canal, but railroads, which were quicker, eventually became the common way for people to travel.

Chicago's growth threatened both the Chicago River and Lake Michigan. The Chicago River ran east and emptied into Lake Michigan, which was the source of the city's drinking water. As the city grew more populous, human and industrial waste polluted the river, which in turn threatened to pollute Lake Michigan. To prevent the drinking water from becoming contaminated, engineers lowered the river bottom in 1871, making the river run backward, or away from the lake.

In 1885 a thunderstorm pushed dirty river water into the lake. Contrary to some inaccurate reports, there was no major outbreak of cholera and typhoid. But there could have been. Alarmed by the potential disaster, city officials made sure the lake water was permanently protected against contamination from the river. In 1900, civil engineers completed the

E 6-28-99

Chicago's 28-mile-long Sanitary and Ship Canal is the only shipping link between the Great Lakes and the Mississippi River. The canal is considered an engineering marvel. It cost over $31 million to construct in 1900. That equals $734 billion in today's money. The American Society of Civil Engineers named the canal the Civil Engineering Monument of the Millennium in 2001.

Chicago Sanitary and Ship Canal. The canal reversed the river's natural flow from eastward to westward. Instead of emptying into Lake Michigan, the water now goes to the Des Plaines River. From there it flows to the Mississippi River, which takes the water to the Gulf of Mexico. The American Society of Civil Engineers has called the successful reversal of the river flow one of the seven engineering wonders of the United States.

Environmentalists have worked hard to clean up the Chicago River to protect the plant and animal life it supports. As noted earlier, many wild onions grow in the area. The marshy

Did You Know?

City Wildlife: Rats

Chicago's least-liked "wildlife" is the Norway rat. It is also called the brown or common rat. This critter is eight inches long. It can swim underwater, fit through a quarter-sized opening, and jump three feet into the air. It will attack people if cornered. The city has established a Target: Rats program to keep the city's rat population under control.

Poison Ivy

Common grackle

land is also home to many **deciduous** (d e h - S I J - e w - u s) trees, such as maple and oak. Wetland grasses are common, but so is poison ivy! Kids who grow up in the Chicago area are taught to avoid the plant, which causes a rash that itches terribly and produces painful blisters.

Although the Chicago River was home to black bears and cougars before European settlers arrived, big predators are now extinct in the city and suburbs. White-tailed deer still find places to live along the riverbank in places where there is a lot of vegetation. Chipmunks, squirrels, raccoons, possum, coyotes, and skunks are commonly seen.

Cardinal

Wild minks are occasionally seen but are more common in less inhabited areas.

In the heart of Chicago you can find many types of songbirds. Colorful robins and cardinals as well as grackles and the wood pewee nest in the city's many parks. Night hawks make nests on the buildings' rooftops. In the spring and fall, thousands of migrating birds pass through Chicago, including purple martins and Canada geese.

Eastern wood pewee

Canada geese in flight

CHICAGO

WRIGLEY FIELD
HOME OF
CHICAGO CUBS

| PIRATES | TOP 9TH | CUBS |
| 1 | | 1 |

Above: The Cubs play a day game at Wrigley Field, the last stadium in Major League Baseball to install lights.

Inset: This well-known sign welcomes fans into historic Wrigley Field.

Right: U.S. President Barack Obama

A City of "Big Shoulders"— People and More

Poet Carl Sandburg, who spent part of his life in Chicago, once described it as the "City of the Big Shoulders." As famous as Chicago is as a center of commerce, transportation, industry, food processing, and shipping, it is also known for its "people" side. This is a side that has produced great art, literature, and music, and that is also rough and tumble—a city that loves its food, sports, and political power.

Located in Cook County, Chicago is divided into fifty wards or districts. The city government consists of a mayor and fifty aldermen, or city council members, one from each ward. The city's most famous mayor was Richard J. Daley, who ran Chicago for twenty-one years, from 1955 until his death in 1976. Daly used his position to influence the national Democratic Party elections by encouraging fellow Democrats to vote. He is credited for helping John F. Kennedy win the 1960 presidential election.

Daley's low point was the 1968 Democratic Convention held in Chicago. It took place at the

Chicago had a reputation as a center of organized crime in the 1920s and 1930s. Two legendary figures from Chicago's past: Gangster Al Capone (left) and federal agent Eliot Ness. From 1929 to 1931, Ness pursued Capone, and story has it that Capone's unsuccessful efforts to bribe Ness's handpicked agents gave birth to the group's famous nickname, "The Untouchables."

height of the antiwar protests over Vietnam. The confrontation between police and protesters turned violent, and the image of police beating unarmed protesters was broadcast on national television. Many Democrats blamed Daley for the bloodshed and for hurting the image of the party. His influence within the party was permanently damaged. In 1972, Democratic Presidential nominee George McGovern kicked Daley out of the Democratic National Convention. Despite that humiliation, Daley was reelected mayor in 1971 and 1975. He died in office on January 20, 1976.

For many years, Richard J. Daley was Chicago's best-known politician . . . until Barack Obama became president of the United States. Although Obama did not grow up in Chicago, he moved there after graduating from Harvard Law School. His wife, Michelle, grew up on the city's South Side. She met Barack Obama at the Chicago law firm where they both worked. Other famous political personalities who were either born in Chicago or have lived much of their lives there include Hillary Rodham Clinton and Jesse Jackson. Before becoming secretary of state in the Obama administration, Clinton was first lady and U.S. senator

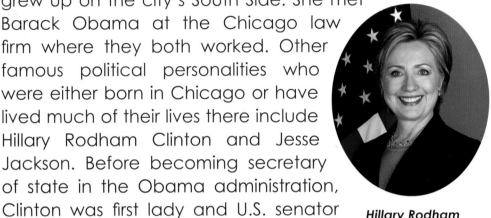

Hillary Rodham Clinton

Richard J. Daley (left) served as mayor longer than any other in the city's history. The current mayor is his son, Richard M. Daley (right), who has held the position since 1989. If he fulfills his current term, he will surpass his father's record.

from New York. Jesse Jackson is a civil-rights activist and, like Clinton, a former candidate for the Democratic presidential nomination.

The best-known Chicagoan of them all is probably Oprah Winfrey. She moved to Chicago in 1983 to

Oprah Winfrey

Michael Jordan

host a local morning TV talk show. Her show was so successful it was broadcast nationally starting in 1986. She is reported to be the wealthiest African American in U.S. history, and the first black female billionaire in the world.

Sports are an integral part of Chicago, and professional teams include the Chicago Bulls basketball team, the Bears football team, the Blackhawks hockey team and two baseball teams: the White Sox and the Cubs. With so many big-league sports teams, Chicago has also been home to many famous athletes. No Chicago athlete is more famous and admired than Michael Jordan, who led the Bulls to six NBA championships.

Chicago has long considered itself an arts and cultural center. The Art Institute was founded in 1879 as both a museum and a school. The Institute's collections include modern European paintings and sculptures, contemporary art, photography, and architecture and design.

The Art Institute is on the western edge of Grant Park, which is often called Chicago's "front yard." In 2001, Millennium Park opened on the northern end of Grant Park. It includes an outdoor music arena, an ice rink, and an underground theater. Millennium Park connects to Grant Park via a winding footbridge 925 feet long.

White Sox mascot Southpaw

Buckingham Fountain is a favorite spot in Grant Park. Its main water jet shoots 150 feet high. At night the fountain is lit by computerized colored lights.

Farther north on Chicago's famous lakefront highway, Lake Shore Drive, is Lincoln Park, the city's largest public park. It has baseball diamonds; volleyball and tennis courts; a botanical garden; a golf course; public beaches; a lagoon; and a zoo. Everyone was surprised to learn that Chicago has the nation's largest

Did You Know?

Cuisine, Chicago-Style

The deep-dish pie known as Chicago-style pizza was invented in 1943 at Chicago's Pizzeria Uno. Deep dish is made with a thick, buttery crust that encircles (like a bowl) toppings usually consisting of cheese, chunky tomato sauce, and other ingredients.

Chicago-style hot dogs usually consist of an all-beef hot dog lying on a poppy seed bun, with yellow mustard, a dill pickle spear, tomato slices or wedges, spicy sport peppers, diced onions, neon-green pickle relish, and a sprinkling of celery salt.

Cloud Gate, a sculpture in Millennium Park, was designed by Indian-British sculptor Anish Kapoor. It is made of 168 stainless steel plates connected with no visible seams.

harbor system, with many marinas and space for more than 5,000 boats! In nice weather, sailboats dot the blue waters of Lake Michigan. By the end of Friday, everyone was excited about the trip on Monday. After the final report was read, Mrs. Thomason congratulated the class: "You all did a great job. Make sure to be here on time Monday morning. The buses leave at seven on the dot."

"Where are we going when we get there?" a student asked.

"Let's keep that a surprise," she smiled, "but here's a clue: We're having pizza for lunch."

The class cheered. Haley looked out the window wistfully. Monday couldn't come fast enough.

Chicago-style hot dog

CHICAGO

Museum Campus Chicago is a lakefront park that extends out into Lake Michigan. It contains Chicago's three most important natural-sciences museums. They are, from front to back, the Field Museum of Natural History, the Shedd Aquarium, and the Adler Planetarium.

Right: A beluga whale, one of the many species of aquatic life at the Shedd Aquarium

Road Trip to Chi-Town

Monday morning was crisp and clear. The school parking lot was empty except for Mrs. Thomason's class. Haley and Klein waited impatiently, bouncing on their toes to stay warm. When the school bus turned into the driveway, the kids cheered. By seven o'clock, they were on their way.

Their first stop was the Shedd Aquarium, at the southern end of Grant Park. Getting off the bus, Haley looked out at Lake Michigan. It was so big that the blue water went on as far as she could see. It reminded her of standing by the ocean.

When the aquarium opened in 1930, one million gallons of ocean water was transported by railroad cars from Florida to create the saltwater exhibits. Haley and her classmates visited each of the permanent exhibits. One was like walking through a flooded **rain forest** with more than 250 species of animals. In another, a diver talked to the class and told them about the different creatures with him in the water. Another exhibit gave them the experience of coral reefs.

The Shedd Aquarium's Oceanarium takes up two levels. At the upper level, visitors sit in the bleachers watching the dolphins do tricks. At the lower level, visitors can watch the dolphins and beluga whales up close as they swim in the tank.

Nobody really knows if Sue, the huge *Tyrannosaurus rex* fossil that greets visitors to the Field Museum, is male or female. She was named after **paleontologist** Sue Hendrickson, who discovered the fossil in 1990 while digging in South Dakota.

A short walk from the aquarium was the Field Museum of Natural History. The first thing the class saw when they walked in was Sue. She stands in the museum's main hallway and is the largest, most complete, and best-preserved *Tyrannosaurus rex* fossil ever discovered. After admiring Sue, Haley and her class went to the Evolving Planet exhibit, which includes the Hall of Dinosaurs.

Pizzeria Uno

They only had time to visit one more exhibit, and the class voted to explore an ancient Egyptian tomb, which belongs to the son of a pharaoh and includes mummified animals as well as people. It was a ten-minute bus ride to lunch at Uno Chicago Grill (which used to be called Pizzeria Uno). Mrs. Thomason ordered Chicago-style deep-dish pizzas. Haley remembered that pizza literally means "pie" in Italian. Her pizza was so thick, she could see why it would be called a pie!

After lunch, everyone got back on the bus to go to Willis Tower. Most Chicagoans still call the building the Sears Tower, which was its original name. When it first opened in 1973, it was the tallest building in the world,

Willis Tower

and it is still the tallest building in the United States. It took a full minute for the fast elevator to reach the Skydeck on the 103rd floor.

The day was so clear and the sun at just the right angle in the sky that Haley could see the shoreline of Lake Michigan north to Wisconsin and south and east to Indiana and Michigan. Her favorite part was also the scariest. She walked onto the glass-bottomed balcony. When she looked down, she could see all the way to the street. It was so far down it made her a little dizzy. It was a windy day, and she could feel the building sway a little!

As they drove along Lake Shore Drive toward the expressway back to Indiana, Haley turned around and watched the Chicago skyline growing smaller. She said a silent good-bye and promised herself she would be back soon.

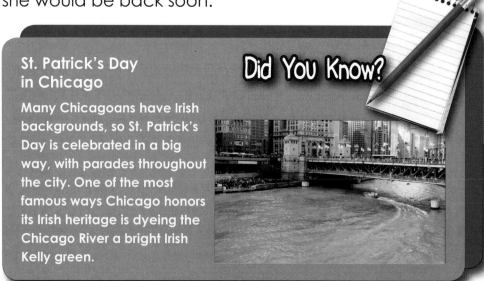

St. Patrick's Day in Chicago

Did You Know?

Many Chicagoans have Irish backgrounds, so St. Patrick's Day is celebrated in a big way, with parades throughout the city. One of the most famous ways Chicago honors its Irish heritage is dyeing the Chicago River a bright Irish Kelly green.

Just The Facts

Location: Northeast Illinois

County: Cook

First European Exploration: 1673, by French Canadians Louis Jolliet and Jacques Marquette

First Permanent Non-Native Settlement: 1781, by Jean Baptiste Point du Sable, of French and Haitian descent

Area: 228 square miles

Population: 2.9 million (city); 9.6 million (metro) (US Census Bureau 2009)

Rank: Third-largest U.S. city by population; twenty-sixth-largest metropolitan area in the world

Highest Point: 735 feet (a landfill on the South Side)

Lowest Point: 577 feet (along the lakeshore)

Annual Precipitation: 33 inches Average

Annual Temperatures: 21°F (January); 73°F (July)

Latitude: 41° 52' 55"N

Longitude: 87° 37' 40"W

Chicago River: 156 miles long

Tallest Building: Willis Tower (former Sears Tower); height: 1,450 feet; stories: 110

Popular Nicknames: The Windy City, The Second City, Chi-Town

Number of Neighborhoods: varies; up to 215 neighborhood names

Major Sports Teams: Chicago Cubs (baseball); Chicago White Sox (baseball); Chicago Bulls (basketball); Chicago Bears (football); Chicago Blackhawks (hockey); Chicago Fire (soccer)

Number of Schools: public: 666; private: 394; colleges and universities: 83

Number of Parks: 552

Daily Newspapers: *Chicago Sun-Times*; *Chicago Tribune*

Major Weekly Newspapers: *Chicago Defender*; *Chicago Reader*

Sister Cities: Accra, Ghana; Amman, Jordan; Athens, Greece; Belgrade, Serbia, Birmingham, United Kingdom; Bogotá, Colombia; Busan, South Korea; Casablanca, Morocco; Delhi, India; Durban, South Africa; Galway, Ireland; Gothenburg, Sweden; Hamburg, Germany; Kiev, Ukraine; Lahore, Pakistan; Lucerne, Switzerland; Mexico City, Mexico; Milan, Italy; Moscow, Russia; Osaka, Japan; Paris, France (partner city); Petah Tikvah, Israel; Prague, Czech Republic; São Paulo, Brazil; Shanghai, China; Shenyang, China; Toronto, Canada; Vilnius, Lithuania; Warsaw, Poland

Make Your Own Chicago-Style Pizza

Like most cities in North America, Chicago loves its pizza. Most Chicagoans will tell you that *their* favorite crust and toppings are what make Chicago pizza great. But when most visitors to the Windy City think of Chicago-style pizza, they think deep-dish. With its hearty, chunky sauce, its piled-on toppings, and its thick, rich crust, Chicago-style pizza is more than a meal—it's an eating experience! Here is a simple recipe you can use to create your own deep-dish pizza with your favorite ingredients.

IMPORTANT NOTE: This project requires the use of sharp utensils to cut food and open cans. It also involves the use of a heated stove. Be sure that an adult is with you at all times to supervise your work and to help you open cans, cut up the food, handle sharp objects, and use the stove.

What You Need:

For the crust:

1 9-inch deep-dish pan OR a square or round baking pan with sides that go up 1-2 inches

1 can (13.8 ounces) of refrigerated "classic" pizza crust (from grocery)

1 teaspoon of olive oil

corn meal

For the sauce:

1 15-ounce can or jar of pizza sauce

1/2 cup of grated Parmesan cheese

For the toppings:
1/4 pound of shredded mozzarella cheese (about 1 cup)
1 pound of cooked Italian sausage (if desired; leave out if you prefer a meatless pizza)
1/2 pound (8 ounces) of thinly sliced pepperoni (if desired; leave out if you prefer a meatless pizza)
1/2 cup of chopped green or red peppers (if desired)
1 cup of sliced mushrooms (if desired)
2 chopped medium plum (Roma) tomatoes (if desired)
1/2 cup of chopped yellow onions (if desired)

What You Do:
1 Heat the oven to 400°F.
2 Brush the bottom of the pan with olive oil.
3 Lightly sprinkle the pan with corn meal.
4 Unroll the dough. Press it in the bottom of the pan and spread it out evenly and up the side of the pan. Dough should extend 1-2 inches up the side of the pan. Fold excess dough under to form crust up the side of the pan.
5 Sprinkle the mozzarella cheese evenly over the bottom of the dough.
6 Spread each of the remaining toppings evenly over the cheese.
7 Pour the pizza sauce over the toppings.
8 Sprinkle the Parmesan cheese evenly over the sauce.
9 Bake until the crust is golden brown, about 20–25 minutes.
10 Remove the pizza from the oven and let it stand for 3–5 minutes.
11 Cut the pizza into large, pie-shaped wedges with a serrated (jagged) knife.
12 Serve and enjoy!

Chicago Timeline

1673   French Canadians Louis Jolliet and Jacques Marquette become the first Europeans to explore present-day Chicago.

1781   The first permanent non-Native settlement is established by Jean Baptiste Point du Sable, who was born in Haiti of French and African descent.

1803   Fort Dearborn is built in the present-day Chicago Loop as a military garrison.

1812   During the War of 1812, when the United States and Britain were at war along with their various Native allies, the U.S. military decides to shut down Fort Dearborn. During the evacuation, the soldiers are attacked by a group of Potawatomis. Although other Potawatomis were said to have advised against the attack, because a number of civilians were killed the Battle of Fort Dearborn also came to be called the Fort Dearborn Massacre.

1837   Chicago is incorporated as a city. By 1840, its population will have grown to 4,000.

1847   The first issue of the *Chicago Tribune* is published.

1855   The Lager Beer Riot grows out of a protest against the arrest of several tavern owners for serving beer on Sunday, resulting in clashes between police and angry citizens.

1860   Abraham Lincoln receives the Republican nomination for U.S. president at the first national convention held by a major political party in Chicago.

1868   The Lincoln Park Zoo is founded as a free zoo. Of the four zoos currently in the Chicago area, this is the only one that lies within the city limits.

1869   The Chicago Water Tower is built.

1871   The Great Chicago Fire breaks out, killing hundreds, leaving tens of thousands homeless, and destroying the entire business district. Immediate efforts to rebuild Chicago lead to the city's becoming one of the largest and most economically successful population centers in the country.

1885   The Home Insurance Building is constructed as part of the rebuilding of Chicago. Because of its height (ten stories), it is known as the world's first skyscraper.

1893   The World's Columbian Exposition, better known as the Chicago World's Fair, is held to celebrate the 400th anniversary of Columbus's voyage to the Americas in 1492.

1900	The flow of the Chicago River is reversed from eastward to westward.
1905	The *Chicago Defender* starts publication; by World War I, it will be the nation's largest and most influential African American newspaper.
1914	Wrigley Field is completed.
1919	In the Black Sox Scandal, a group of Chicago White Sox players conspire with known gamblers to intentionally lose the World Series to the Cincinnati Reds. (Cincinnati wins, five games to three.)
1924	Grant Park Stadium (Soldier Field), the future home of the Chicago Bears of the NFL, is completed.
1929	The St. Valentine's Day Massacre: On February 14, members of a gang led by mobster Bugs Moran are gunned down in a garage, presumably by killers either belonging to or hired by rival Al Capone's gang.
1930	The Shedd Aquarium opens. It is the first inland aquarium with a permanent saltwater fish collection.
1934	The Brookfield Zoo opens.
1948	The first issue of the *Chicago Sun-Times* is published.
1955	Richard J. Daley is elected mayor of Chicago.
1968	Demonstrators protesting the war in Vietnam clash with police at the Democratic National Convention.
1973	The Sears Tower is completed; it is the world's tallest building.
1976	Richard J. Daley dies in office.
1989	Richard M. Daley becomes mayor.
2000	The Field Museum unveils Sue, the largest, most complete, and best-preserved *Tyrannosaurus rex* fossil ever discovered.
2007	Richard M. Daley is elected to his sixth term as mayor.
2008	President-elect Barack Obama gives his acceptance speech in Chicago's Grant Park.
2009	The Sears Tower is officially renamed Willis Tower.
2010	The Chicago Bulls meet the Cleveland Cavaliers in the NBA Eastern Conference playoffs. Wrigley Field remains the oldest ballpark in the National League.

Further Reading

Books

Bielski, Ursula. *Creepy Chicago: A Ghosthunter's Tales of the City's Scariest Sites*. Chicago: Lake Claremont Press, 2003.

Chicago Tribune (staff files). *Chicago Days: 150 Defining Moments in the Life of a Great City*. New York: McGraw-Hill, 1996.

Christopher, Matt, and Glenn Stout. *Matt Christopher Legends in Sports: Michael Jordan*. Boston: Little, Brown, 2008.

Dybek, Stuart. *The Coast of Chicago: Stories*. New York: Picador, 2004.

Grossman, James R., Ann Durkin Keating, and Janice L. Reiff (editors). *The Encyclopedia of Chicago*. Chicago: University of Chicago Press, 2004.

Jones, Jen. *Celebrities with Heart: Oprah Winfrey*. Berkeley Heights, New Jersey: Enslow Publishers, 2010.

McNulty, Elizabeth. *Chicago Then and Now*. San Diego: Thunder Bay Press, 2000.

Zschock, Martha Day. *Journey Around Chicago From A To Z*. Beverly, Massachusetts: Commonwealth Editions, 2005.

Internet Sources

Chicago History Museum
   http://www.chicagohistory.org/

The Chicago Park District
   http://www.chicagoparkdistrict.com/index.cfm/
   fuseaction/root.home/intHomeLink/1/home.cfm

Explore Chicago: Chicago for Kids
   http://www.explorechicago.org/city/en/things_see_do/
   tours/tourism/chicago_for_kids_audio.html

The Field Museum
http://www.fieldmuseum.org/

The Shedd Aquarium
http://www.sheddaquarium.org/

A View on Cities: Chicago History
http://www.aviewoncities.com/chicago/chicagohistory.htm

Willis Tower
http://www.willistower.com/

Works Consulted

Abu-Lughod, Janet L. *New York, Chicago, Los Angeles: America's Global Cities.* Minneapolis: University of Minnesota Press, 1999.

Anderson, Dale. *The FBI and Organized Crime.* Broomall, Pennsylvania: Mason Crest Publishers, 2010.

Barrett, James R. *Work and Community in the Jungle: Chicago's Packinghouse Workers 1894–1922.* Chicago: University of Illinois Press, 1987.

Gropman, Donald. *Say It Ain't So, Joe!: The True Story of Shoeless Joe Jackson.* New York: Carol Publishing Group, 1995.

Halper, Albert, editor. *The Chicago Crime Book.* Cleveland: World Publishing Co., 1967.

Husband, Joseph. *The Story of the Pullman Car.* Chicago: A. C. McClurg & Co., 1917.

Glossary

abundantly (uh-BUN-dunt-lee)—In great numbers; a lot.

adaptation (aa-dap-TAY-shun)—The act of changing something to suit another use.

deciduous (deh-SIJ-ew-us)—(of trees or other plants, especially hardwood trees) Shedding leaves during winter and growing them back in spring.

descent—The family origins or background of an individual.

fertile (FUR-tuhl)—Capable of growing crops.

humid—Having a relatively high amount of water vapor in the atmosphere.

incorporated (in-KOR-pur-ay-ted)—Formed; organized.

manufacturing (man-yoo-FAAK-chur-eeng)—Making something on a large scale, usually using machines.

marshes—Grassy wetlands, usually located between dry land and a body of water.

metropolis (meh-TRAH-puh-liss)—A big city and its surrounding areas.

migrate—To move from one region or habitat to another.

plains—Mostly flat, treeless countryside, unique to the United States; prairies.

rain forest—A dense forest, rich in a wide variety of plant and animal species, usually found in tropical areas with consistently heavy rainfall.

skeptically (SKEP-tik-lee)—Showing signs of having doubts or of not being easily convinced.

sleet—Frozen rain or a similar form of freezing precipitation, often mixed with rain or snow.

species—A group of similar animals, plants, or other living organisms that are capable of reproducing among themselves.

Index

ABOUT THE AUTHOR

Kathleen Tracy has been a journalist for over twenty years. Her writing has been featured in magazines including *The Toronto Star*'s "Star Week," *A&E Biography* magazine, *KidScreen*, and *TV Times*. She is also the author of numerous books for Mitchell Lane Publishers, including *The Fall of the Berlin Wall; Paul Cézanne; The Story of September 11, 2001*; and *Class Trip: San Diego*. Tracy grew up 40 miles from the Chicago Loop and while in grade school regularly visited the city on weekend family excursions. The summer before moving to California to attend UCLA, Tracy worked at the Holiday Inn on Lake Shore Drive and spent most lunch breaks in one of the city's many parks. Her favorite places included the Egyptian exhibit at the Field Museum, Grant Park, and Wrigley Field, where she attended the Cubs' opening home game every year until moving to California.